THE BEATLES

FOR EASY CLASSICAL GUITAR

T0021140

ARRANGED BY MARK PHILLIPS

ISBN 978-1-4803-6865-1

HAL•LEONARD®
CORPORATION
7777 W. BLUEMOUND RD. P.O. BOX 13819 MILWAUKEE, WI 53213

And I Love Her

Words and Music by
John Lennon and Paul McCartney

Moderately

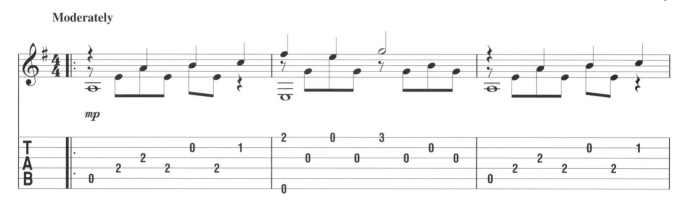

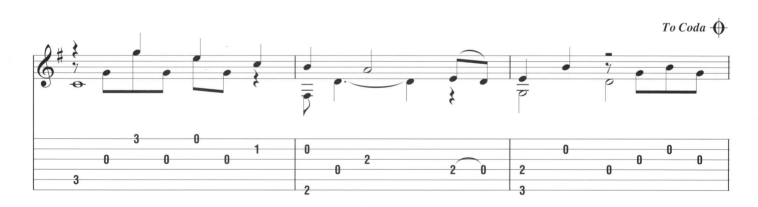

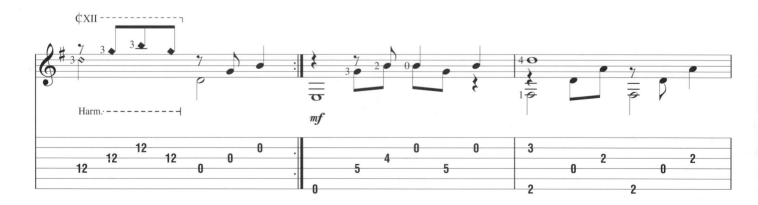

D.C. al Coda

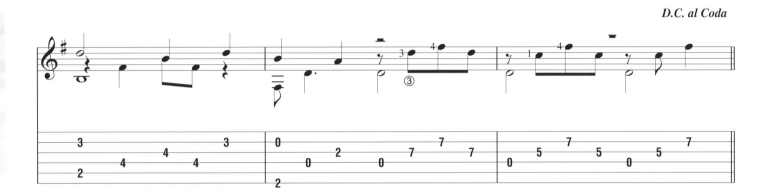

Coda

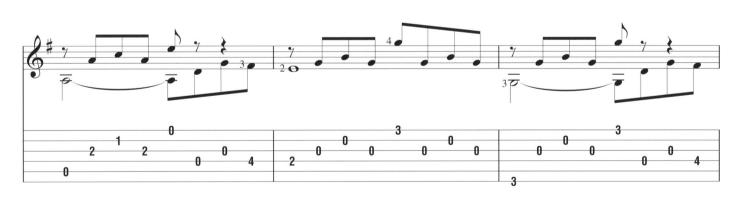

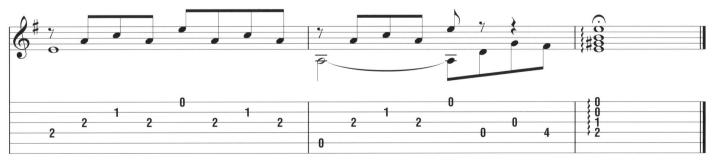

Baby's in Black

Words and Music by
John Lennon and Paul McCartney

Moderately slow, in 2

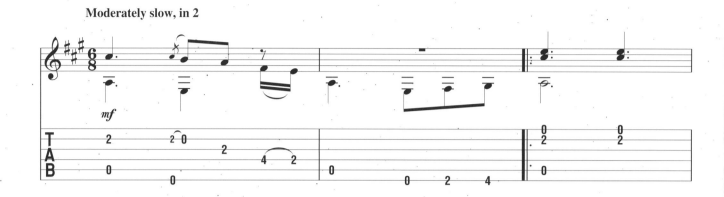

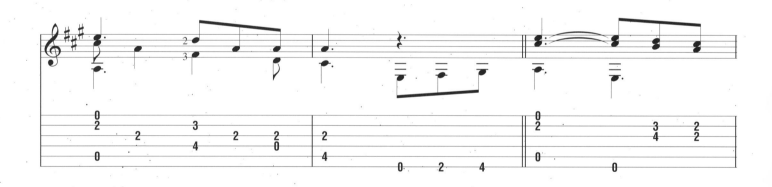

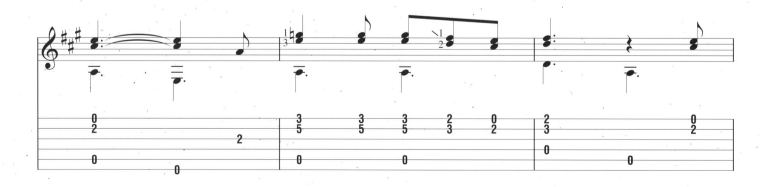

Because

Words and Music by
John Lennon and Paul McCartney

Moderately slow

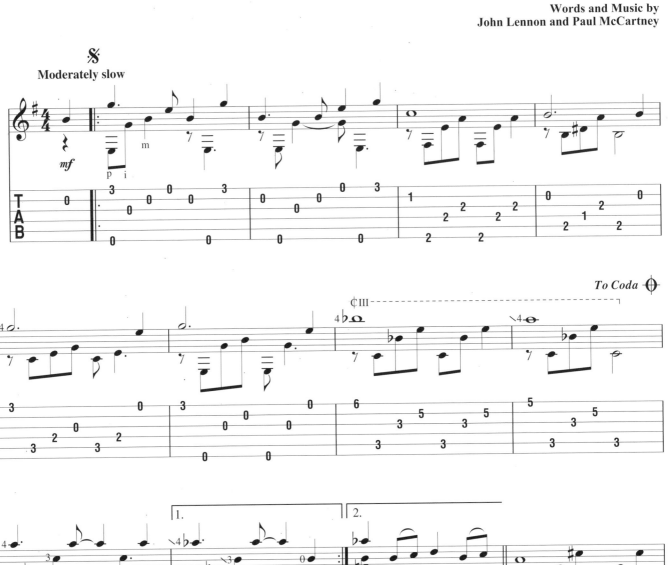

I Will

Words and Music by
John Lennon and Paul McCartney

Moderately

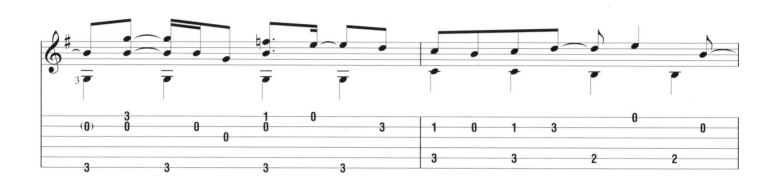

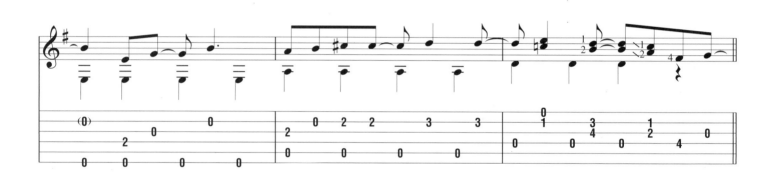

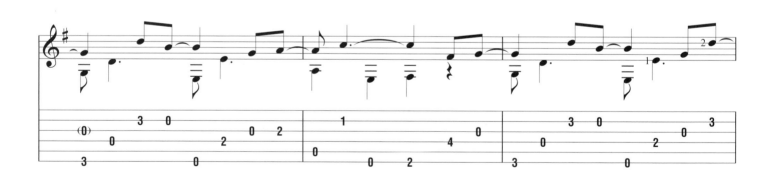

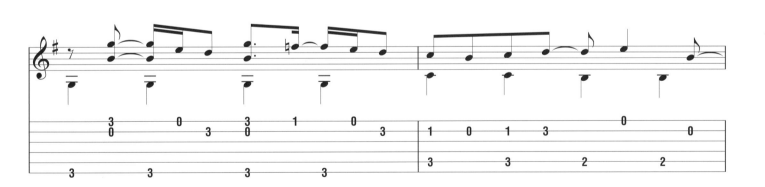

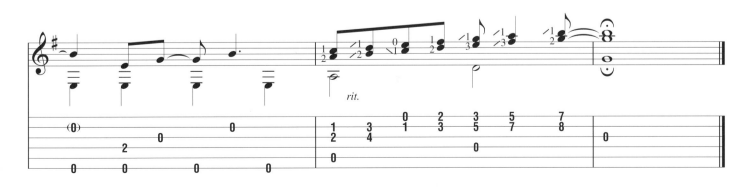

Do You Want to Know a Secret?

Words and Music by
John Lennon and Paul McCartney

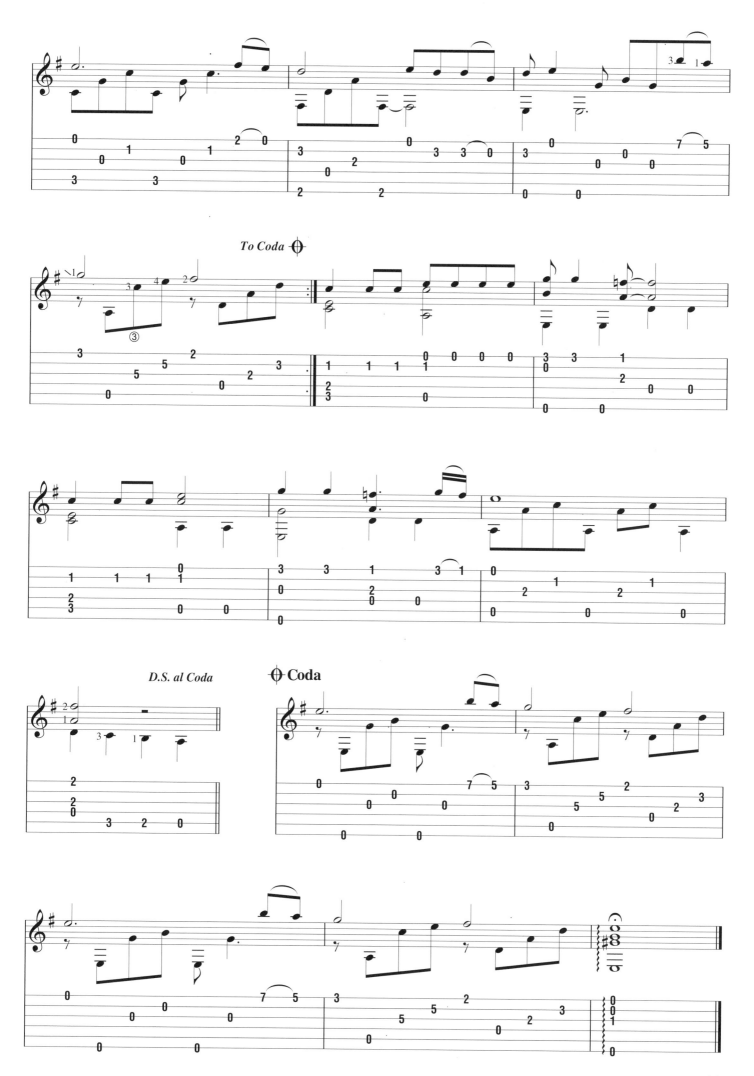

Eleanor Rigby

Words and Music by
John Lennon and Paul McCartney

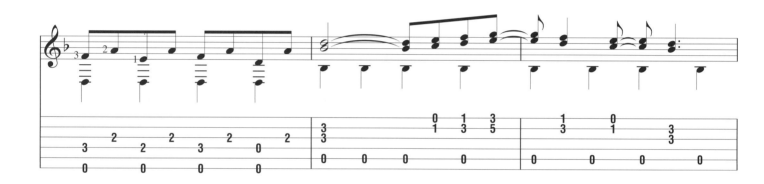

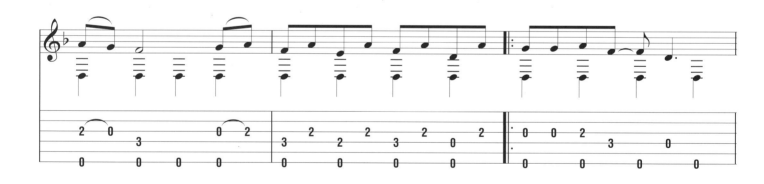

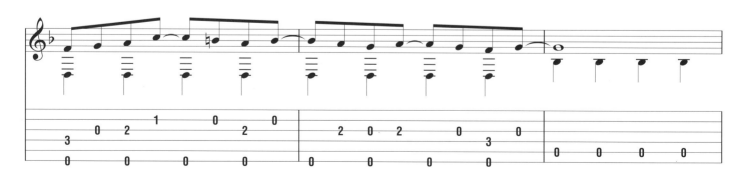

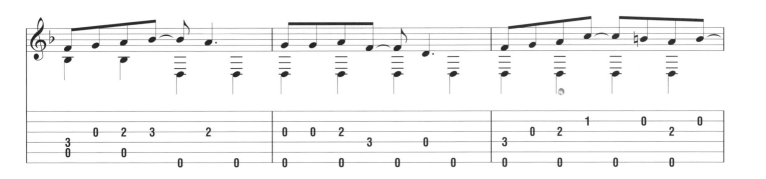

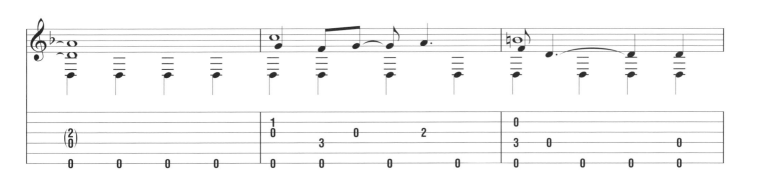

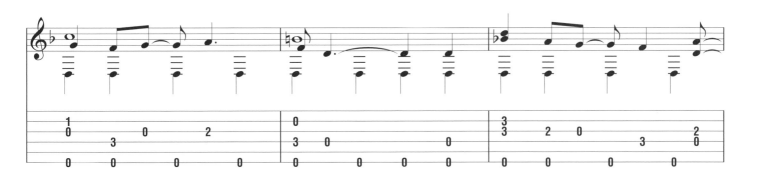

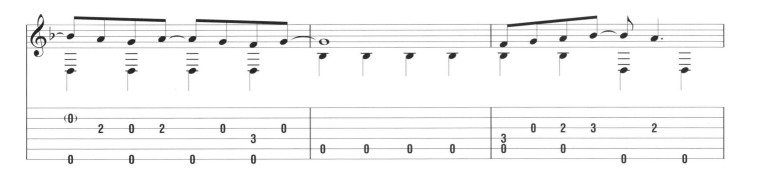

To Coda ⊕ *2nd time, D.C. al Coda*   ⊕ **Coda**
          (no repeat)

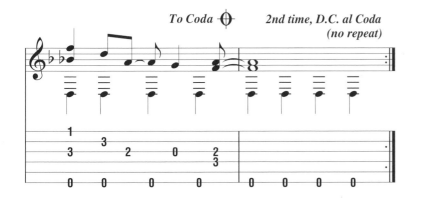

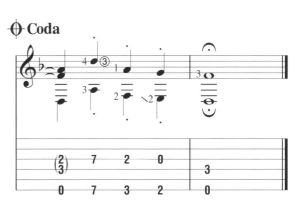

Here, There and Everywhere

Words and Music by
John Lennon and Paul McCartney

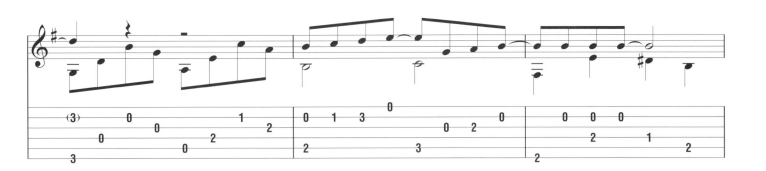

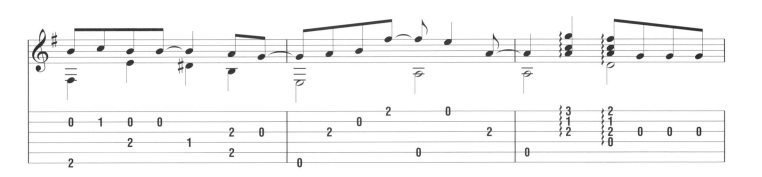

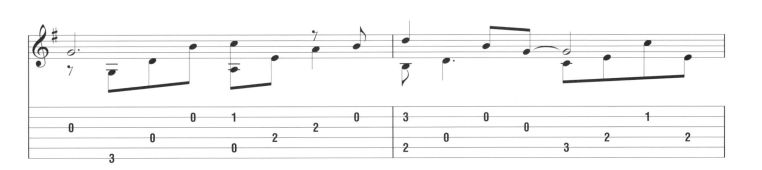

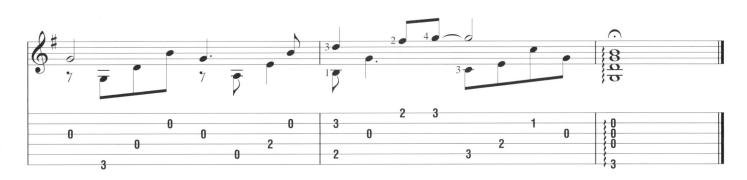

Hey Jude

Words and Music by
John Lennon and Paul McCartney

D.S. al Coda
(no repeat)

Coda

If I Fell

Words and Music by
John Lennon and Paul McCartney

If I Needed Someone

Words and Music by
George Harrison

Moderately fast

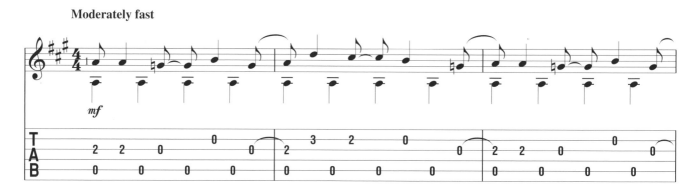

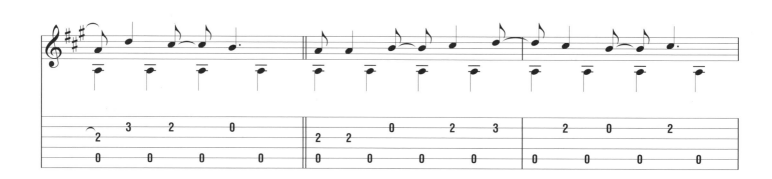

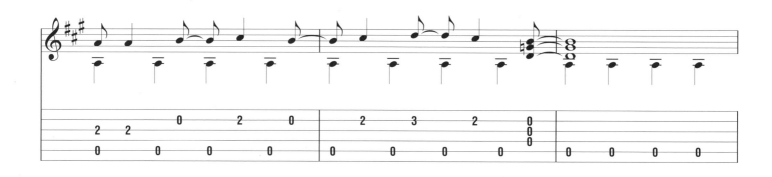

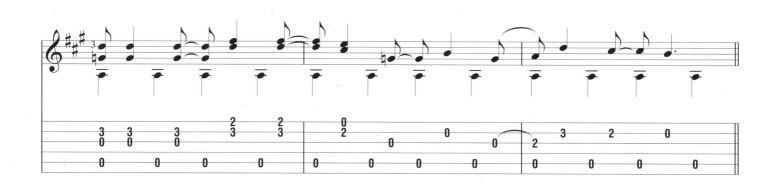

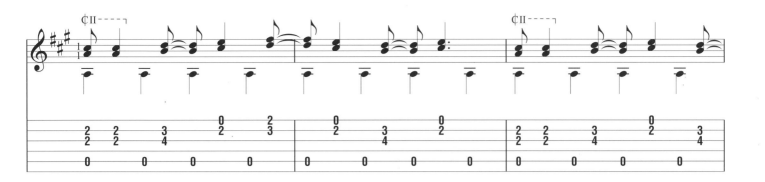

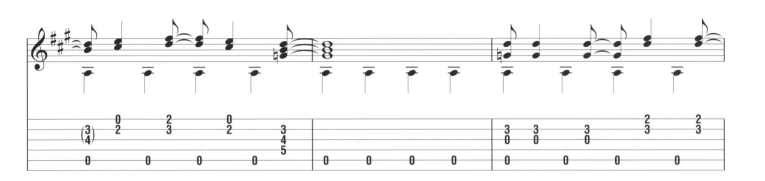

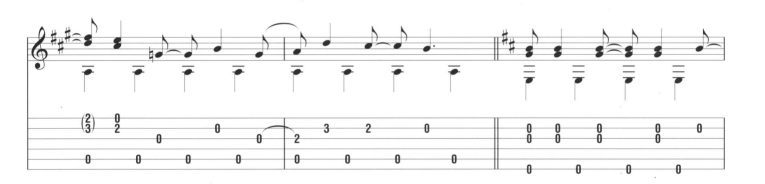

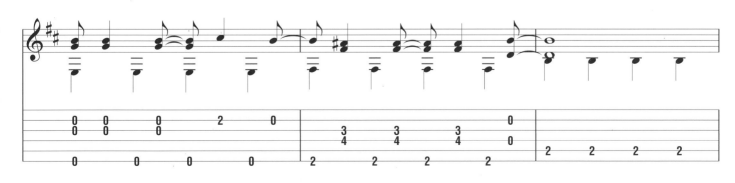

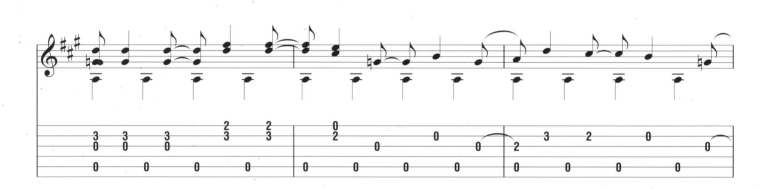

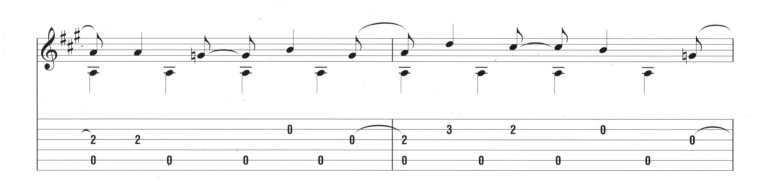

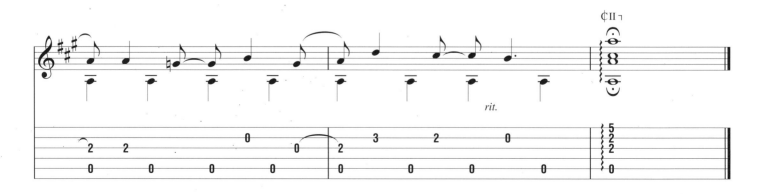

Michelle

Words and Music by
John Lennon and Paul McCartney

23

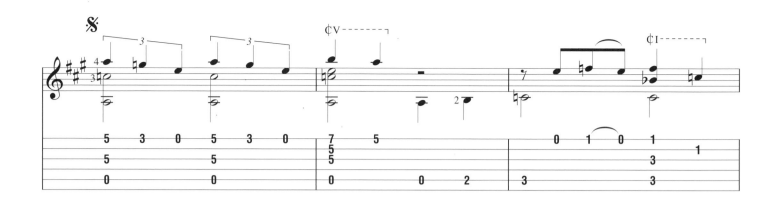
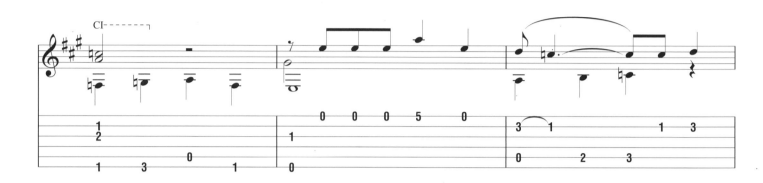
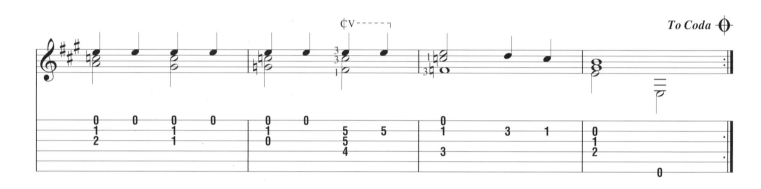
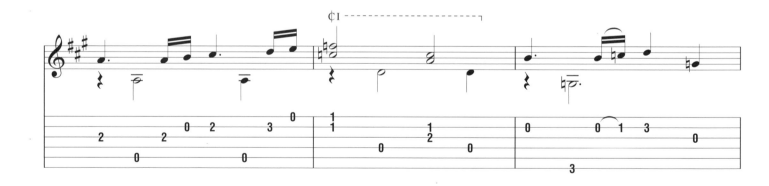
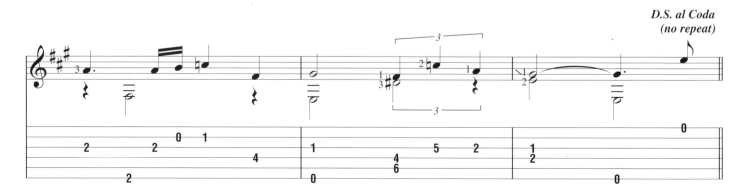

Coda

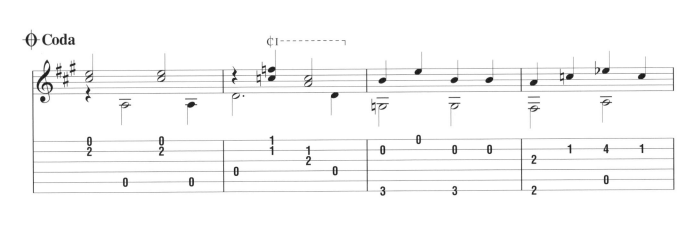

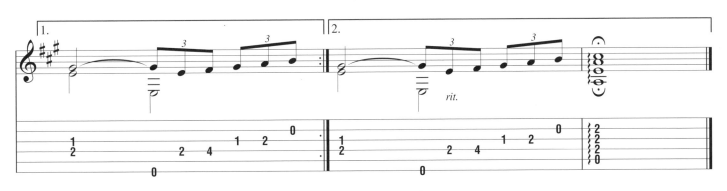

In My Life

Words and Music by
John Lennon and Paul McCartney

Moderately

It's Only Love

**Words and Music by
John Lennon and Paul McCartney**

Moderately

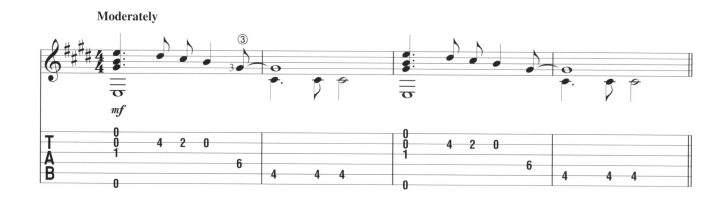

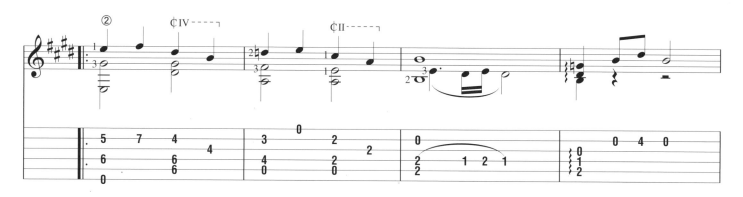

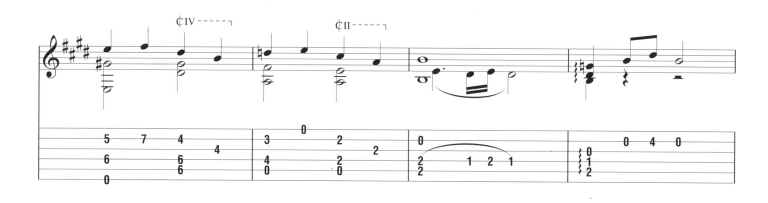

Let It Be

Words and Music by
John Lennon and Paul McCartney

Moderately

The Long and Winding Road

Words and Music by
John Lennon and Paul McCartney

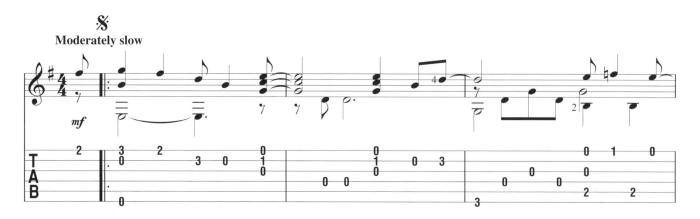

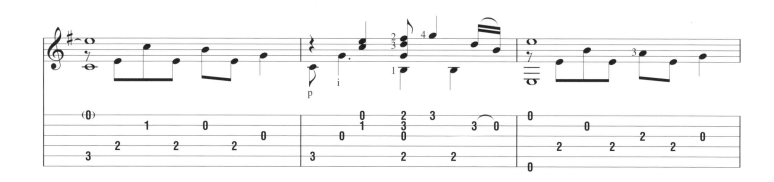

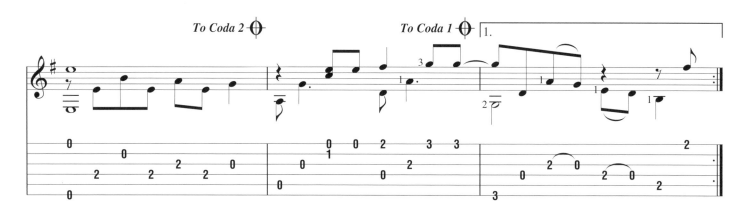

Mother Nature's Son

Words and Music by
John Lennon and Paul McCartney

Slowly

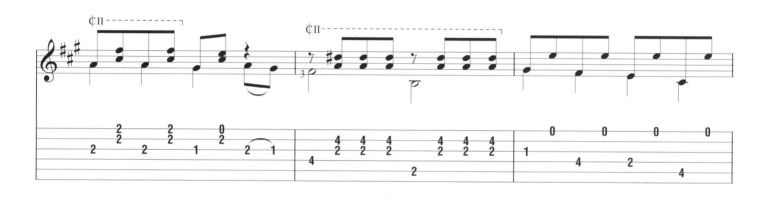

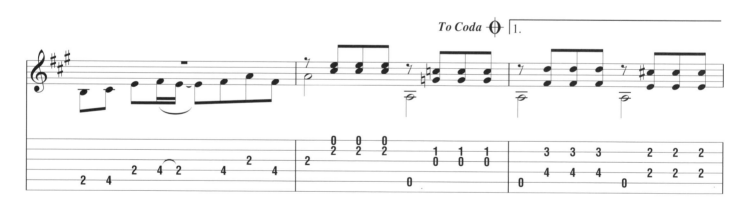

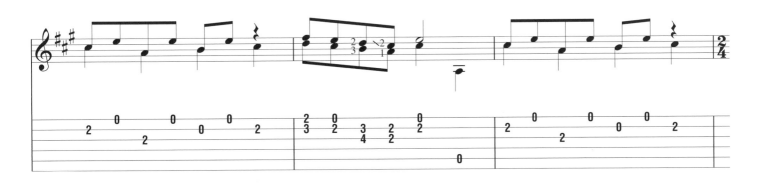

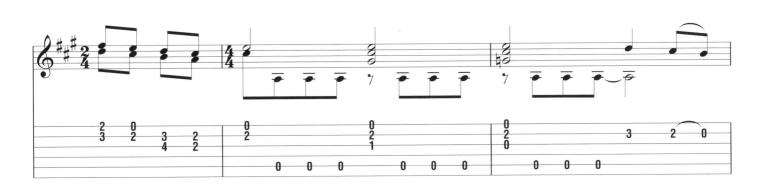

D.C. al Coda
(no repeat)

⊕ Coda

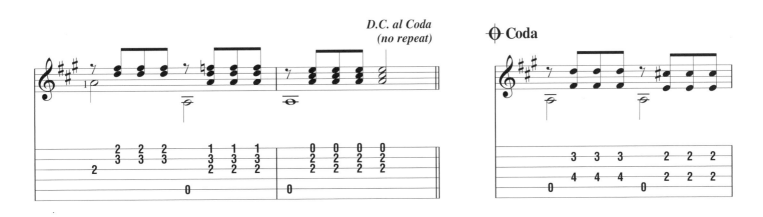

rit.

Nowhere Man

Words and Music by
John Lennon and Paul McCartney

2nd time, D.C. al Coda

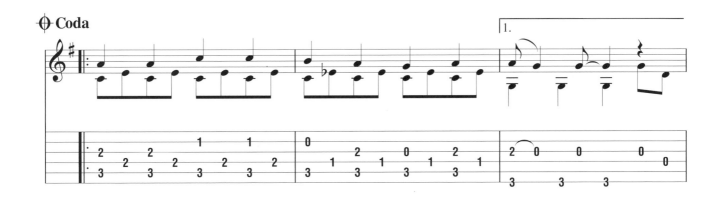

Coda

P.S. I Love You

Words and Music by
John Lennon and Paul McCartney

We Can Work It Out

Words and Music by
John Lennon and Paul McCartney

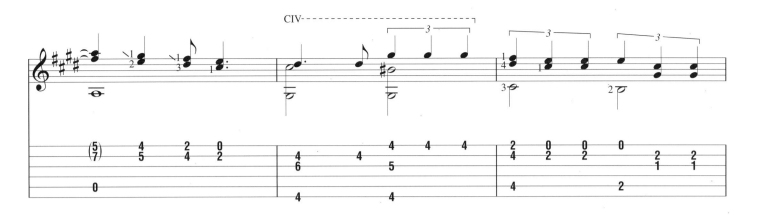

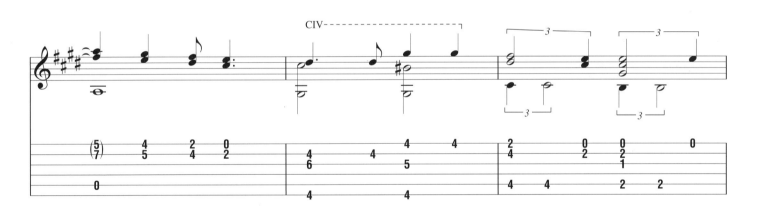

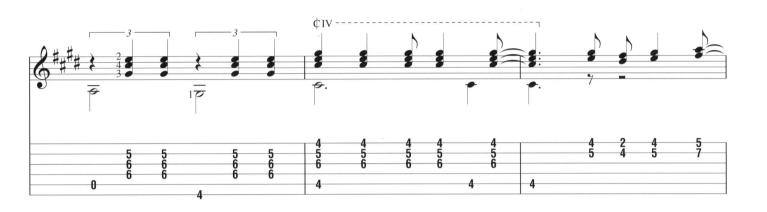

D.C. al Coda
(no repeat)

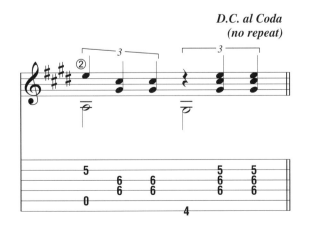

⊕ **Coda**

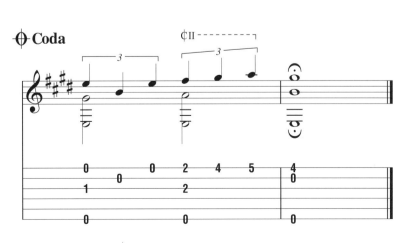

With a Little Help from My Friends

Words and Music by
Joh Lennon and Paul McCartney

Moderately, in 4

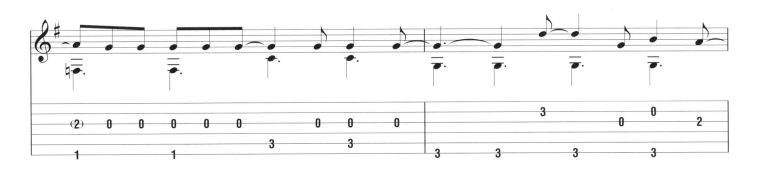

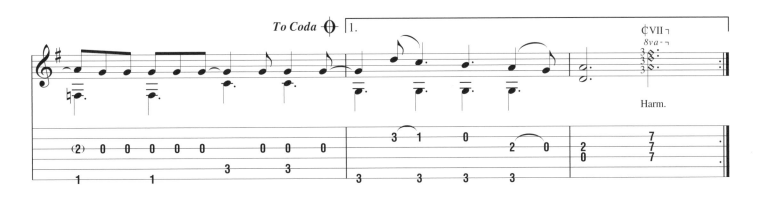

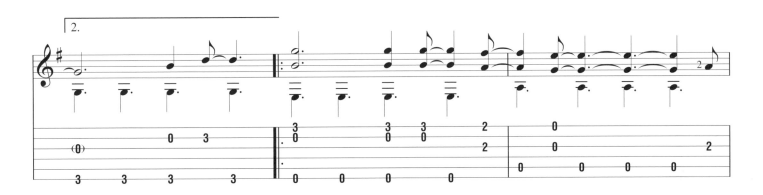

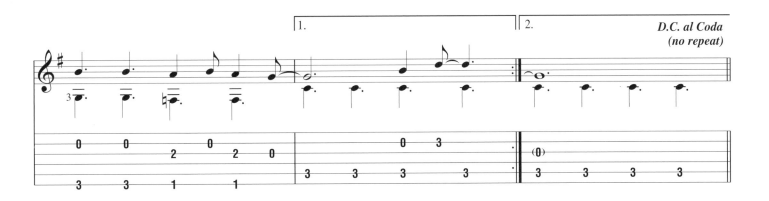

You Won't See Me

Words and Music by
John Lennon and Paul McCartney

Yesterday

Words and Music by
John Lennon and Paul McCartney

Moderately slow

FINGERPICKING GUITAR BOOKS

Hone your fingerpicking skills with these great songbooks featuring solo guitar arrangements in standard notation and tablature. The arrangements in these books are carefully written for intermediate-level guitarists. Each song combines melody and harmony in one superb guitar fingerpicking arrangement. Each book also includes an introduction to basic fingerstyle guitar.

    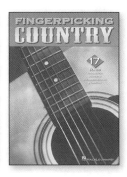 

Fingerpicking Acoustic
00699614 15 songs......................$14.99

Fingerpicking Acoustic Classics
00160211 15 songs......................$16.99

Fingerpicking Acoustic Hits
00160202 15 songs......................$12.99

Fingerpicking Acoustic Rock
00699764 14 songs......................$14.99

Fingerpicking Ballads
00699717 15 songs......................$14.99

Fingerpicking Beatles
00699049 30 songs......................$24.99

Fingerpicking Beethoven
00702390 15 pieces.....................$10.99

Fingerpicking Blues
00701277 15 songs $10.99

Fingerpicking Broadway Favorites
00699843 15 songs......................$9.99

Fingerpicking Broadway Hits
00699838 15 songs......................$7.99

Fingerpicking Campfire
00275964 15 songs......................$12.99

Fingerpicking Celtic Folk
00701148 15 songs......................$10.99

Fingerpicking Children's Songs
00699712 15 songs...................... $9.99

Fingerpicking Christian
00701076 15 songs......................$12.99

Fingerpicking Christmas
00699599 20 carols......................$10.99

Fingerpicking Christmas Classics
00701695 15 songs......................$7.99

Fingerpicking Christmas Songs
00171333 15 songs......................$10.99

Fingerpicking Classical
00699620 15 pieces.....................$10.99

Fingerpicking Country
00699687 17 songs......................$12.99

Fingerpicking Disney
00699711 15 songs......................$16.99

Fingerpicking Early Jazz Standards
00276565 15 songs $12.99

Fingerpicking Duke Ellington
00699845 15 songs......................$9.99

Fingerpicking Enya
00701161 15 songs......................$16.99

Fingerpicking Film Score Music
00160143 15 songs......................$12.99

Fingerpicking Gospel
00701059 15 songs......................$9.99

Fingerpicking Hit Songs
00160195 15 songs......................$12.99

Fingerpicking Hymns
00699688 15 hymns $12.99

Fingerpicking Irish Songs
00701965 15 songs......................$10.99

Fingerpicking Italian Songs
00159778 15 songs......................$12.99

Fingerpicking Jazz Favorites
00699844 15 songs......................$12.99

Fingerpicking Jazz Standards
00699840 15 songs......................$10.99

Fingerpicking Elton John
00237495 15 songs......................$14.99

Fingerpicking Latin Favorites
00699842 15 songs......................$12.99

Fingerpicking Latin Standards
00699837 15 songs......................$15.99

Fingerpicking Andrew Lloyd Webber
00699839 14 songs......................$16.99

Fingerpicking Love Songs
00699841 15 songs......................$14.99

Fingerpicking Love Standards
00699836 15 songs $9.99

Fingerpicking Lullabyes
00701276 16 songs......................$9.99

Fingerpicking Movie Music
00699919 15 songs......................$14.99

Fingerpicking Mozart
00699794 15 pieces.....................$9.99

Fingerpicking Pop
00699615 15 songs......................$14.99

Fingerpicking Popular Hits
00139079 14 songs......................$12.99

Fingerpicking Praise
00699714 15 songs......................$14.99

Fingerpicking Rock
00699716 15 songs......................$14.99

Fingerpicking Standards
00699613 17 songs......................$14.99

Fingerpicking Wedding
00699637 15 songs......................$10.99

Fingerpicking Worship
00700554 15 songs......................$14.99

Fingerpicking Neil Young – Greatest Hits
00700134 16 songs......................$16.99

Fingerpicking Yuletide
00699654 16 songs......................$12.99

Order these and more great publications from your favorite music retailer at
halleonard.com

Prices, contents and availability subject to change without notice.

  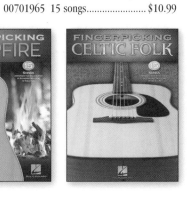   

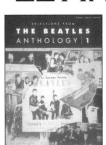
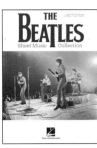
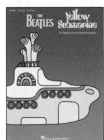
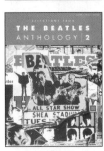
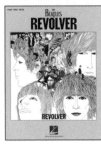